The
World's
Stupidest
Chat-Up
Lines

The World's Stupidest Chat-Up Lines

Michael O'Mara Humour

First published in Great Britain in 2005 by
Michael O'Mara Books Limited
9 Lion Yard, Tremadoc Road
London SW4 7NQ

Copyright © Michael O'Mara Books Limited 2005

A CIP catalogue record for this book is available
from the British Library

ISBN 1-84317-019-1

1 3 5 7 9 10 8 6 4 2

Designed and typeset by K DESIGN, Winscombe, Somerset

Written and compiled by Chris Maynard and Rhian McKay

Printed and bound in Great Britain by Cox & Wyman Ltd,
Reading, Berkshire

www.mombooks.com

Contents

I came, I saw, I pulled

Introduction

*T*he scene is all too familiar; Helen of Troy or Adonis enters the room, your eyes meet theirs and the chemistry sends shivers down your spine and makes your pulse beat faster. Your options are clear: make the move and instigate a conversation that could soon have you laughing and loving in giddy succession, or nail your feet to the floor and tell yourself, 'next time'.

Well, shape up – *now* is the next time.
Walk the walk, and talk the talk.

Of course, these things don't *always* go to plan. We can't guarantee that these chat-up lines will hook your desired one, but, one way or another, you can be sure you'll get a reaction. Whether you favour the cheesy opening line to get a laugh, or the smooth-as-silk compliment to sweep them off their feet, *The World's Stupidest Chat-Up Lines* will provide you with more material than we hope you'll ever need. And, if you're the recipient of some of these howlers, we sympathize – you'll be grateful for the section of scathing put-downs that will halt a would-be *amour* at fifty paces.

Love waits for no one – your soulmate is standing there, in anticipation. Go get 'em, tiger!

Adonis

Helen of Troy

7

Cheesy Chat

*Y*our first port of call – these cheesy lines brilliantly combine a piercing insight into the opposite sex with subtle compliment. Well, perhaps that's not *strictly* true. They may, in fact, result in you being shot a look of intense disapproval, with a healthy dose of insufferable pity, just for having the brazen audacity to use one. But until you try them out, who knows? Go on, we dare you...

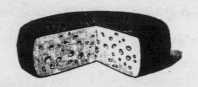

Do you have a map? Because
I keep getting lost in your eyes.

❤

Did you just grab my bum?
No? Well, you can if you want to.

❤

I know we've only just met,
but I've just come back from
the future where we're having
a passionate love affair.
And it started tonight.

If I could rewrite the alphabet,
I would put U and I together.

♥

Excuse me, do you have
a phone I can borrow?
I told my mother I'd call her when
I met the woman of my dreams!

It's not my fault I fell in love.
You're the one who tripped me.

Somebody call the police!
It must be against the law
to look as good as you.

❤

Can you tell me the time?
I want to make a note of the
moment we first met.

❤

You must be from Jamaica,
because Jamaican me crazy.

Helen of Troy was so beautiful
the Trojans got into a horse.
You're so beautiful I'd get into a Trojan.

♥

I'm not usually this tall.
I'm sitting on my wallet.

♥

When God made you,
he was showing off.

Hi, I suffer from amnesia.
Do I come here often?

❤

You are the shining star that completes
the constellation of my existence.

Is your daddy a thief?
So who was it that stole the stars from
the sky and placed them in your eyes?

❤

Did the sun come out or did
you just smile at me?

❤

Darling, you're so sweet, you
put Nestlé out of business.

❤

There's only one thing your eyes
haven't told me – your name.

Darling, if I had you, I wouldn't
have to dream any more.

♥

So, what are the chances that
we can engage in anything more
than conversation tonight?

You must be going to Hell, because
it's surely a sin to look so good!

So, are you going to kiss me, or
do I have to lie to my diary?

❤

Do you believe in love at first sight,
or should I walk by again?

❤

Have you always been this gorgeous
or is it something you work at?

Will you treat me like a tent
and put me up for the night?

❤

Are you a parking ticket?
Because you've got fine
written all over you.

❤

I can't wait till tomorrow.
Because I bet you become
even more beautiful with
every passing day.

If I pet you, would
you follow me home?

❤

I must be lost, angel –
I thought Paradise was further south.

I've lost my teddy bear.
Can I cuddle you instead?

I had a dream and you were it.

❤

When I look into your eyes
I can see our future.

❤

What's your parents' number?
I need to call them
and thank them for having you.

Er…I'm very rich.

❤

I see my reflection in your eyes,
and you can keep my soul.

❤

I didn't know angels
could fly so low!

Do you have a doggie bag?
I want to take you home with me.

❤

Excuse me but I think I just
dropped something! My jaw!

❤

Don't tell anyone else –
I'm naked under these clothes!

If you were a tear in my eye
I would not cry for fear of losing you.

❤

Do you have any raisins?
Well, how about a date then?

❤

Do you know how much a
polar bear weighs?
No, nor do I, but it broke the ice.

You see my friend over there?
[Point to your sheepish-looking
friend, who waves for effect.]
He/she wants to know if you think
I'm cute.

❤

Is it hot in here or is it just you?

❤

You're so sweet, I'm worried that just by
kissing you my teeth will fall out.

I need someone really bad.
Are you really bad?

♥

Are you religious? Good, because
I'm the answer to your prayers.

You can call me Fred Flintstone,
because I'm going to make your
bed rock.

Was your dad a king for a day?
He must have been to have made
a princess like you.

Did you get your knickers from
outer space? Because your
bum is simply out of this world.

If I told you that you had a beautiful
body, would you hold it against me?

Baby, if you were a laser gun…
you'd be set on stun.

❤

Were you in the Boy Scouts/
Girl Guides? Because you've
tied my heart in knots.

❤

Well, here I am.
What are your other two wishes?

You are the reason women/men
fall in love.

♥

Have you got a calculator?
I need to work out just
how much I fancy you.

♥

The best part of me is covered up.

So, how was Heaven when you left?

❤

Excuse me, do you mind if
I stare at you for a minute?
I want to remember your
face for my dreams.

❤

Hi – what would you like for
breakfast tomorrow morning?

I bet you a hundred pounds
that you won't kiss me.

❤

Excuse me, but is your last
name 'Gillette', 'cos you're the
best a man can get!

❤

Poor you!
How are you coping with
that terrible fever?
[I haven't got a fever!]
No? It's just that you look hot to me.

[With your hands on his/her shoulders]
Oh, these are shoulder blades?
I could have sworn they were wings.

♥

Are you hurt?
Because down here's a
long fall from Heaven.

♥

Excuse me, do you have the time?
Because I've got the energy.

Is there an airport nearby or
is that just my heart taking off?

❤

Is your father a mechanic?
Then how did you get such
a finely tuned body?

You can fall off a building or
out of a tree, but the best way
to fall is in love with me.

Can I have directions, please?
[To where?]
Why, your heart, of course.

❤

I was sitting here holding
this drink when I realized
I'd rather be holding you.

❤

Your eyes are blue, just like the ocean.
And baby, I'm drowning.

If your parents hadn't met I'd be
a very unhappy man right now.

♥

I feel like Richard Gere standing here,
next to you, Pretty Woman.

♥

[While studying his/her upturned hands.]

THE SEVEN PRINCIPAL LINES.

1. LINE OF HEART.   2. LINE OF HEAD.   3. LINE OF LIFE.
4. LINE OF SATURN.   5. LINE OF THE SUN.   6. LINE OF THE LIVER.
7. VENUS'S RING.

I can read palms and yours says you've
just met the partner of your dreams.

Was your father an alien?
Because there's nothing else
like you on earth!

❤

I hope you know CPR, because you
just take my breath away.

❤

I'm sorry – were you talking to me?
No? Well, please start.

Is your surname Jacob's?
Because you're a real cracker!

♥

If you were a new hamburger at
McDonald's, you'd be a McGorgeous.

♥

Didn't anyone tell you that
you wanted to sleep with me?
I'm sorry, I thought you knew...

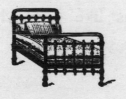

You must be great at fishing 'cos you've
caught me hook, line and sinker.

Does God know he's missing an angel?

Would you like to try an Australian kiss?
It's just like a French kiss,
but down under...

You look like my first wife.
[Really? How many times have you
been married?]
Oh, I'm still a bachelor.

❤

Get your coat love, you've pulled.

❤

Excuse me, but your flies are undone.
Oh, maybe not now, but definitely later.

Quick, call an ambulance!
The sight of you has stopped my heart!

❤

There must be something wrong with
my eyes – I can't take them off you.

❤

Do you mind if I stare at you
from up close instead of from
across the room?

Are your eyes bothering *you*?
They're bothering me.

I think I could fall madly into
bed with you.

♥

Do you want to snog?
I need to know whether you
taste as good as you look.

Don't you know me
from somewhere?

♥

Congratulations! You've been voted
'Most Beautiful Girl In This Room',
and the grand prize is a night with me!

♥

What would you say
was the best thing about
being so gorgeous?

Quick, someone call Heaven,
there's an angel on the loose!

❤

Can I have a picture of you?
I want to show Santa Claus
what I'd like for Christmas.

❤

Am I dead, angel?
Because this must be Heaven!

Are you here alone, or will someone have to win your affections over my dead body?

I've had a really bad day and it always makes me feel better to see a pretty girl smile. So, would you smile for me?

❤

I've always been fascinated by beautiful women. Do you mind if I study you closely?

Just call me vitamin C.
I'll do your body good.

♥

I looked up 'sexy' in the
dictionary today and there you were.

♥

Are you going to give
me your phone number
or am I going to
have to follow you home?

I'm on a sponsored snogathon
for charity – would you
like to boost my total?

♥

Here's my phone. Call your
flatmate and tell them you
won't be home tonight.

Do you believe in helping the
homeless? Yes? Well, let me
come home with you then.

Are you from Tennessee?
Because you're the only ten I see!

❤

Are you lost?
Because Heaven's a
long way from here.

❤

Is there a doctor in the house?
Because I think I twisted my ankle
when I fell for you.

Pardon me, I seem to
have lost my phone number,
could I use yours?

❤

Can I call you [name]?
Really, what time?

❤

Excuse me, does my tongue
taste funny to you?

[Lick your finger and press it on
their shirt, then on yours.]
Oh dear, let's get out of these wet clothes.

❤

That dress looks great on you...
as a matter of fact, so would I.

❤

If I were a gardener,
I'd plant your tulips next to mine.

Hi, I'm Mr Right. Someone
said you were looking for me?

❤

I'm fighting the urge to make
you the happiest woman on
earth tonight.

❤

If you're going to regret this
in the morning, we can sleep
in till the afternoon.

You look so familiar to me;
weren't we lovers in a previous life?

❤

Is that a fox on your shoulder,
or am I seeing double?

❤

I'll buy you dinner if you
make me breakfast.

Sleazy Spiel

*R*ight, so the cornball approach didn't work? Perhaps, then, it's time to substitute sultry for sleazy? Sexy for sordid? It's guaranteed you'll get the laughs, and with the right partner it may go down like a dream…of course, so may you when a well-aimed right hook connects with your jaw. Well, as they say, love hurts…

Have you ever been to the moon?
No, well come sit on my rocket and
I'll take you there and back.

❤

What has sixty teeth and holds back
the Incredible Hulk? My fly.

❤

The only thing I want to come
between you and me is a condom.

Hey, my shoes are having a party –
would your dress like to come down
and join them?

♥

Do you want to go back to my
place for sex and coffee?
No? You don't want coffee?

People tell me I've got a one-track
mind, but that track is heading
straight for you, babe. Shall we pull
into the sidings and couple?

Hi, I'm a sex bomb.
Defuse me!

❤

Hello, are you here to meet a
nice boy/girl? Or will I do?

❤

What do you say to
going behind a rock and
getting a little boulder?

You look a little pale.
Luckily I've brought my flesh
thermometer with me.

❤

Screw me if I'm wrong, but I think
you want to sleep with me.

❤

Let's play pool. We can use my
cue and balls, and your holes.

As you've lost your virginity,
can I play with the box it came in?

❤

If I flip a coin, what are the chances
of me getting head?

❤

Do you know what's fantastic in bed,
is hung like a horse, and winks?
No?
[Cue sly wink.]

Hi, I'm an organ donor, and I have
an organ I think you might need.

You remind me of a spanner.
Every time I see you my nuts tighten.

❤

I bet you fifty pounds that
you can't get all your clothes
off in two minutes.

If you've been bad go to your room.
If you want to be naughty come to mine.

♥

Hey, darling, let me slay
you with my love sword.

♥

You know, love is a little like
photography – best developed
in the dark.

My magic watch says you're not
wearing any underwear. You are?
Oh, I guess it must be an hour fast then.

Do you know the essential difference
between sex and conversation?
You don't? Well, let's go upstairs
and have a chat then.

♥

Excuse me, do you have sex with strangers?
No? Then allow me to introduce myself.

You look like someone with taste.
Would you like to taste me?

❤

Those clothes are very becoming
on you, but if I were on you,
I'd be coming too.

❤

It's not the size of the boat –
it's the motion of the ocean...

Let's go back to my place and
do all the things I'll tell everyone
we did anyway.

♥

Put your crash helmet on, love.
You'll be going through the
headboard later.

♥

How do you feel about going
halves on a bastard?

Was your father a farmer?
Because you have lovely melons.

♥

Was your mother a baker?
Because you have great buns.

Does your father mix cement?
Because you're making me hard.

Are you free some time next week?
Or do you charge?

❤

Hey – how do you like your eggs in
the morning? Poached, scrambled
or fertilized?

❤

Is your father a chicken farmer?
Well, you sure know how to
raise cocks.

Flawed Flattery

*T*his section is for the truly masochistic – when the straightforward approach doesn't work, why not try some of these for a more 'oblique' take on the flirting business? After opening with a truly backhanded compliment, watch as your potential date wrestles with bewilderment, and then sit back and observe the fireworks. They'll either be impressed with your bald-faced honesty and mature, up-front approach – at which point the game of love can continue – or they'll get their mates over to sort you out.

You may not be the best-looking
girl here, but beauty is only a
light switch away.

♥

The attraction I feel for you is like
diarrhoea. I just can't hold it in.

♥

I'm a hedge, and you look like
a horse. Care to jump me?

I may not be the best-looking
guy hcrc, but I'm the only one
talking to you.

You're ugly, but somehow erotic.

❤

The voices in my head told me
to come and talk to you.

Don't you worry. I go more for personality than for looks.

♥

You don't sweat much for a fat girl.

♥

You look great. Will you refer me to your plastic surgeon?

I'm curious to know if you're as good in bed as all the other guys say you are!

❤

I just wanted to tell you I think your dancing is amazing. It's like when you're out there you don't care what anybody thinks, which is great!

❤

Hi. You'll do.

I'd love to have a long, hot, steamy
shower with you.
Because you smell really bad.

I want to know all about you.
Starting with why you have that
stupid look on your face.

❤

Did your face get all bashed up
when you fell from Heaven?

You're ugly, but you intrigue me.

♥

I just had to find out what
kind of person would go out
dressed like that...

♥

What's a nice girl like you
doing in a body like that?

You want to see some magic?
Let's go back to your place tonight and in
the morning I'll disappear for ever!

❤

I've just been dumped and I'm sure
you can make me feel better.

❤

You look like my ex, only uglier.

I'm sure you didn't mean to
turn me on with your big ass,
but it's too late now!

♥

You know, the more I drink,
the more attractive you get!

You look like you're pretty experienced.
Want to teach me a thing or two?

Have you heard that things
go stiff when they're dead?
Well, put your hands down my
trousers and you'll see I'm dying.

❤

Wow, you look like a million dollars.
All green and wrinkled.

❤

I'd like to shag you senseless, but it
looks like someone got there first.

It's great you have big feet –
I like stability.

❤

I think you're the most
beautiful girl I've ever seen...
on a Wednesday.

❤

If you were a bogey,
I'd pick you first.

Punchy Put-downs

*A*s the Boy Scouts say, be prepared. This is never truer than in the chat-up game, when the lack of a pithy comeback or suitably withering response may leave you saddled with a complete loser for the entire evening. Learn how to puncture not only their advances but their egos too with these scathing put-downs.

Is this seat empty?

Yeah, and this one will be too if you sit down.

❤

You probably think it's a bit odd me coming up to you like this, but I had a strange desire to buy you a drink.

I don't want anything to do with your strange desires.

❤

So, let's skip the awkward beginning and pretend we've known each other for ages. How's the family?

They told me never to see you again.

Fancy a shag?

No thanks, I've already got one arsehole in my knickers.

❤

You know, I think the colour of your hair is wonderful.

Thank you. It's on aisle three in the chemist down the road.

❤

I know I'm not a library book so why do you keep checking me out?

I'd go through anything for you.
OK, let's start with your bank account.

Man: So, what do you do for a living?
Woman: *I'm a female impersonator.*

❤

Would you like to dance?
No.
You must have misheard me –
I said you look fat in those pants.

I can tell that you want me.
Yes, I want you to leave.

❤

Can I come back to your place?
Yes, if I can go to yours.

❤

I hoped I'd meet the partner
of my dreams tonight.
*Oh yes? I'll just go and see if
I can find them for you.*

May I have the last dance?
You've just had it.

♥

Your placc or mine?
Both. You go to your place,
and I'll go to mine.

♥

When I look at you,
I know I've caught the love bug.
That doesn't look like the only
disease you've got.

So, would you like to come back
to my place?
Well, I don't know.
Will two people fit under a rock?

❤

I want to give myself to you.
Sorry, I don't accept cheap gifts.

❤

You've got the face of an angel.
Yeah? Well, you've got the face of a saint.
A Saint Bernard.

Hey, come on, let's be honest – we're both at this bar for the same reason.
Yeah! Let's pick up some girls!

❤

I know how to please a woman.
Then please leave me alone.

❤

Who chose your outfit?
Stevie Wonder?

Haven't I seen you somewhere before?
Yeah, that's why I don't go there any more.

♥

You look like a dream.
Go back to sleep.

♥

What sign are you?
No entry.

Don't you think it was fate
that brought us together?
No, just bad luck.

♥

You seem familiar.
Have we met in a previous life?
*Yes, and I didn't want anything
to do with you then, either.*

♥

How did you get to be
so beautiful?
*God clearly gave me
your share of the
attractiveness genes.*

I would go to the end of
the world for you.
Yes, but would you stay there?

♥

What's it like being the most beautiful
boy/girl in this bar?
What's it like being the biggest
liar in the world?

♥

Oh God, look at you!
Was anyone else hurt in the accident?

Cyber Chat

*F*or the technologically savvy out there, this section's for you. Whether you're wooing over the web, or just interested in keeping up with the latest developments in online dating, you'll find everything you need in here. Beware however, the photo of that gorgeous guy or gal you're conversing with may not accurately represent the final product...

Do you want to
crash at my place?

♥

So, do you need a
hot-male account?

♥

Do you .com here often?

CnIBrw10p2CLYaMa2ThnkHr?

Your homepage or mine?

♥

What's a nice url like you doing
in a place like this?

♥

Your Windows are like eyes
into your soul.

CnIFlrtWivU?

Don't you think we just click?

❤

You're the attachment
I've been looking for.

❤

I have some raw code
I'd love to try your compiler on.

DrpM!

Want to come and see my hard drive?
I promise it's not 3½ inches and
it certainly ain't floppy.

❤

You make my software
turn to hardware!

❤

I think my attachment will
fit nicely into your port.

ImNtLOkin4ARltnshpImLOkin4AnXprnce

Nice Legs!

*I*t's time to talk specifics, and when you're paying her legs as much attention as these lines demonstrate, she won't fail to be flattered.

If you believe that, you'll believe anything...

If your left leg was Easter,
and your right leg was Christmas,
could I meet you between
the holidays?

❤

Nice legs.
What time do they open?

❤

Is that a ladder in your stocking
or the stairway to Heaven?

Your legs remind me of the flu.
I hope they spread as easily.

❤

The word of the day is 'legs',
so let's go back to my place
and spread the word.

❤

I'd like to wrap your
legs around my head and wear
you like a feed bag.

I wanna use your thighs
as earmuffs.

♥

Your legs must be tired,
because you've been running through
my mind all night!

♥

You have incredible legs –
would you mind if I took
them home with me?

Just where do those
legs of yours end?

♥

So, darling.
Do you want to know why
they call me tripod?

♥

Your legs are like softened butter.
Smooth, creamy and easy to spread.

Smooth Seduction

*O*K, hands up – who flicked to this section first? Hoping to charm a way into the desired's affections along the cool, calm and sophisticated route has always been a popular choice, and these chat-up lines will serve to make most of you as irresistible as you are resourceful (you bought this book, didn't you?). We emphasize – most of you...

Do you have a boyfriend? Well, when you want a MANfriend, come and talk to me.

❤

Your name must be Daisy, because I have the incredible urge to plant you right here.

❤

Those are nice jeans. Do you think I could get into them?

That's a nice dress.
Any chance I can talk you out of it?

❤

I like maths. How about we go to my
room, add the bed, subtract your clothes,
divide your legs and multiply?

❤

Congratulations, beautiful,
you're the next contestant in the
Game of Love, and I'm your host.

You know, you might be asked
to leave soon. You're making
the other women/men in this
bar look really bad.

♥

I think you would look especially
beautiful with your eyes closed...
in my bed.

♥

Baby, you're so hot you'd
make the Devil sweat.

You have such beautiful long blonde
hair; it would look lovely spread
across my pillow.

❤

I've been noticing you not noticing me.

❤

I had a dream about you last night.
Let's go back to my place and
make it a reality.

Hey, all those curves,
and me with no brakes!

❤

If I were to ask you for sex,
would your answer be the same
as the answer to this question?

❤

Quick, call the cops.
Someone just stole my heart!

Have you ever kissed a rabbit
between the ears?
[Pull your trouser pockets inside out.]
Would you like to?

❤

Would you like someone
to mix with your drink?

❤

The next item up for auction
is in my trousers.

Shall we talk now,
or just continue flirting from a distance?

❤

May I end this sentence
with a proposition?

❤

What are you doing at two o'clock
tomorrow morning?

Did you hear the latest health reports?
You need to increase your
daily intake of vitamin *Me*.

❤

Aren't we supposed to
get together for a candlelight
dinner later tonight?

❤

Damn, sugar, settle down. I'm diabetic.

My face will be departing
in half an hour.
Care to ride on it?

❤

You like my name?
You should hear my phone number!

❤

Hey baby! You've got it going on,
now how 'bout I see it coming off?

[Grab someone's bum.]
Pardon me, is this seat taken?

❤

Anything drugs can do,
I can do with my tongue.

❤

Is your father
a forest ranger?
Because whenever
I look at you,
I get wood in my pants.

Since wastage is inexcusable
in this day and age, what do
you say we use these condoms
in my pocket before they expire?

❤

If you want me, don't wake me,
or shake me, just take me.

❤

Excuse me, do we have a mutual
friend who could introduce us?

Do you know what'd look
good on you? Me.

♥

You know what I like about you?
My arms.

♥

Help me, I'm lost.
Which way is it to your place?

Do you sleep on your stomach?
Can I?

❤

Would you like to have
breakfast tomorrow?
Should I call you or nudge you?

❤

Do you have a temperature
or are you always this hot?

My name's [name],
but you can call me 'lover'.

♥

I've got these lovely new
satin sheets and no one to
share them with...

♥

Are we related?
Do you want to be?

Are you looking for Mr Right,
or Mr Right Now?

♥

That dress would look great
on the floor next to my bed.

♥

I know a great way to
burn off the calories you
just drank in that drink.

You'll be on my mind this
Valentine's Day, but I'd prefer
you in my bed.

My name's [name].
That's so you know what to scream.

❤

Excuse me, is that dress felt?
Would you like it to be?

I'm sorry, we don't
allow clothes in here.

❤

Can you believe that just a
few hours ago we'd never even
been to bed together?

❤

I play the field and it looks like
I just hit a home run with you.

What's a nice girl/guy like you
doing in a place like this?

❤

I wonder what our
children will look like?

❤

This Valentine's Day I want you
to know that I'll be head-over-heels
for you – and I know some other
positions too!

Crude Come-ons

*I*f you've made it this far, pack your bags and get ready to board with the other losers on your one-way journey to Heartbreak Hotel. However, you've got one more chance to turn things around, a last gasp attempt at salvaging your pride (and, getting lucky...) – and it's come to this. The 'Crude Come-ons'. Well, they're good for a laugh at least. Only the foolhardy and the thick-skinned need apply...

You know, I'd give you a piece
of my mind, but I've got so much
more of something else.

♥

[In your best pirate voice]:
I must be huntin' treasure,
'cos I'm diggin' yer chest!

♥

I'm a gynaecologist.
How long has it been since
your last check-up?

There's a party in your
mouth and I'm coming.

❤

Can you drive? Well,
back on to this!

❤

Excuse me, I think I left my
wallet in your pocket.
Just let me check.

You know, you've got the
prettiest teeth I've ever dreamed
of coming across.

❤

Say – do you want to see
something really swell?

❤

Want to play 'Lion'? It's a
game where you get down
on all fours and growl while
I feed you the meat.

I'm a helicopter pilot.
Do you fancy a ride on my chopper?

❤

You remind me of a squirrel.
I'd like to pile my nuts up against you.

❤

Let's play 'Carpenter'! First we get
hammered, and then I nail you.

If I gave you a sexy negligee,
would there be anything in it for me?

❤

I can read you like a book.
I reckon you're great between
the covers.

❤

Is my underwear showing?
No?
Would you like it to be?

No, that's not a gun in my pocket.
I *am* happy to see you.

❤

I would kill or die to make love
to you. Sex is a killer... want
to die happy?

❤

Yeah, be careful, it's big and
if you stroke it, it spits.

Do you have a mirror in your pocket, because I can see myself in your underwear!

♥

I love every bone in your body – especially mine.

♥

You have pretty eyeballs.
Of course, they'd be nicer if they were eyeing my pretty balls.

What do you say we go back to my place and play 'Soldier'? I lay down and you blow the hell out of me.

♥

Fancy quitting this joint? I know where there's a good party; they've got liquor in the front, and poker out the back.

♥

Do you want to play 'Boxing'? We square up and you give me a few blows.

I wish you were a door so
I could bang you all day long.

❤

Let's play *'Titanic'*.
When I shout 'Iceberg!', you go down!

❤

I know you want to
come home with
me tonight. I've got
a six-inch tongue and
I can breathe through
my ears.

Are you cold? You should be;
you've been naked in my
mind all night.

❤

I've got a condom with
your name on it.

❤

If you look that good in
clothes, I bet you look
even better out of them.

Do you have any Italian
[German, Swedish, Irish etc.] in you?
Would you like some?

❤

How would you like to see
the soles of your shoes in
my wing mirrors?

❤

Would you like to be my love buffet?
I'd lay you out on the table
and take what I want.

Why don't you come over
here, sit on my lap, and
we'll talk about the
first thing that pops up.

❤

I'm a pilot. Care to
experience some thrust?

❤

Hi, do you dissect insects for
scientific research? No? I thought
you might like to look inside my fly.

Hi, I've lost my virginity.
Can I have yours?

❤

You've got a great smile,
but it's a shame it's not the
only thing you're wearing!

❤

Smile. It's the second best thing
you can do with your lips.

Michael O'Mara Humour

All Michael O'Mara titles are available by post from:
Bookpost, PO Box 29, Douglas, Isle of Man, IM99 1BQ

Credit cards accepted.   Telephone: 01624 677237   Fax: 01624 670923
Email: bookshop@enterprise.net   Internet: www.bookpost.co.uk

Free postage and packing in the UK.
Other Michael O'Mara Humour titles: